...E BATS, GIANT INSECTS,

AND OTHER MYSTERIOUS ANIMALS OF THE

DARKEST CAVES

EXTREME ANIMALS IN EXTREME ENVIRONMENTS

ANA MARÍA RODRÍGUEZ

E Enslow Publishers, Inc.
40 Industrial Road
Box 398
Berkeley Heights, NJ 07922
USA

http://www.enslow.com

For my husband and sons, who share my journeys through extreme worlds

Acknowledgments

The author expresses her immense gratitude to the scientists who so kindly gave their time to comment on the manuscript and provided images to illustrate the book. Your help has been extremely invaluable.

Library of Congress Cataloging-in-Publication Data

Rodriguez, Ana Maria, 1958–
    Vampire bats, giant insects, and other mysterious animals of the darkest caves / Ana María Rodríguez.
        p. cm. — (Extreme animals in extreme environments)
    Includes bibliographical references and index.
    Summary: "Explains why caves are extreme environments and examines how vampire bats, giant water bugs, and other animals have adapted to the harsh conditions"—Provided by publisher.
    ISBN 978-0-7660-3698-7
    1. Cave animals—Juvenile literature. 2. Caves—Juvenile literature. I. Title.
    QL117.R63 2012
    591.75'84—dc22

                    2010037577

Paperback ISBN 978-1-4644-0018-6

ePub ISBN 978-1-4645-0468-6

PDF ISBN 978-1-4646-0468-3

Printed in the United States of America

092011 Lake Book Manufacturing, Inc., Melrose Park, IL

10 9 8 7 6 5 4 3 2 1

Illustration Credits: © Alan Cressler, pp. 4, 10, 11 (top), 12, 14, 18, 31, 33, 38; Michael Tobler, Oklahoma State University, pp. 35, 36; Organization for Bat Conservation, pp. 1, 21, 22, 25; Peter Arnold Images / Photolibrary, p. 26; Peter Jones, National Parks Service, p. 11 (bottom); © 2011 Photos.com, a division of Getty Images. All rights reserved, p. 15; Robert Pickett / Papilio, pp. 3, 28; Shutterstock.com, p. 7.

Cover Illustration: Organization for Bat Conservation (Vampire bat).

CONTENTS

"Stephen discovered underground rivers in Mammoth Cave. He saw eyeless fish swimming in them. No one had heard of such creatures. Scientists came from all over the world to study them"[1]

—"Stephen Bishop: Cave Explorer," by Judith Boogaart

1
ENTER THE CAVE WORLD

Caves are home to bizarre creatures. Take blind fish, for example, like the one Stephen Bishop caught in an underground river in Mammoth Cave, Kentucky. Stephen Bishop was a slave owned by Franklin Gorin, who also owned Mammoth Cave. In the 1830s, Gorin opened the cave to visitors and placed seventeen-year-old Stephen Bishop as the tour guide.

But he was much more than a guide. He was so curious and courageous that he found and explored more underground passages and chambers than any other guide of his time. Many consider him the first American cave explorer. Bishop called Mammoth Cave "grand, gloomy, and peculiar," and the cave stands true to its name. According to the U.S. National Park Service, Mammoth Cave has about 390 miles (628 kilometers) of passages explored, which makes it the longest known cave system in the world.[2]

THE MYSTERIOUS WORLD UNDERGROUND

Cave exploration, or spelunking, is popular all over the world. Cave explorers, or cavers, climb up or down, rappel, crawl on mud, dive in dark water, wade, or walk for miles to reach these underground worlds. Caves are extreme environments for animals mainly because they are totally dark and may have very limited food supplies.

Caves are cold and humid. The temperature varies little compared to the temperature outside the cave. In summer, caves are cooler than outside and in winter they provide a warmer environment. About 15 percent of our planet's land is shaped by caves and similar land features, such as sinkholes, springs, and blind valleys.[3]

HOW CAVES FORM: SOLUTION CAVES AND LAVA TUBES

Water carves rocks and forms caves. Caves are mostly in a type of rock called limestone. Limestone is made primarily of a mineral called calcite. Calcite does not dissolve in pure water, but dissolves quickly in acidic water.[4] (Acids taste bitter. Vinegar and lemon juice are examples of mild acids).

Most large caves are "solution caves." They form when acidic water seeps through cracks or pores (minute holes) on the surface of

Caves are mostly made up of a type of rock called limestone. This is the inside of a limestone cave in South Africa.

CAVE FACTS

✦ Many caves are formed in landscapes called karst. The word comes from *Kras*, a region in Slovenia with abundant limestone landscapes carved with deep caves.[5] Karst is a landscape characterized by rock that can be dissolved by weak acids. This process helps the formation of caves and underground streams.

✦ Caves have few or many chambers connected by intricate passages. Passages can be large enough for people to walk through. Others can be narrow and small, forcing cavers to crawl or drag their bodies. Underground rivers may flow through caves, and lakes flood parts of or whole chambers. Some caves have one or more natural openings. Others have been totally isolated from the surface world for thousands or maybe millions of years until humans found them, usually by accident.

✦ Cave chambers come in all sizes and shapes. Some have room enough to fit the largest aircraft.[6]

✦ Some caves are underwater, and cavers need to use diving equipment to reach them. The "cenotes" (se-NO-tays) of the Yucatán Peninsula are hundreds of water-filled sinkholes surrounded by thick jungle vegetation.[7]

✦ Besides caves, aquifers form another important subterranean habitat for underground wildlife. Aquifers are layers of rock, sand, or gravel through which enough water flows to supply wells and springs. Some aquatic cave invertebrates and vertebrates live mostly in aquifers.

the ground. The water is acidic because it contains carbonic acid. Some of the carbonic acid forms in rainwater when it picks up carbon dioxide (CO_2) from the atmosphere. The acid dissolves calcite, which enlarges existing fissures or cracks on rocks. Carving a cave by this process may take tens of thousands of years, or even millions of years. Mammoth Cave, the one explored by Stephen Bishop, was formed this way. McDougal's Cave, which is described in Mark Twain's *The Adventures of Tom Sawyer*, is a real solution cave located near Twain's hometown of Hannibal, Missouri.[8] The actual cave has about two miles of zigzagging passages.

There are places where a stronger acid forms, called sulfuric acid. In this case, microbes living deep inside the ground transform hydrogen sulfide (H_2S) into the acid. Because sulfuric acid is stronger than carbonic acid, it carves bigger caves faster. Famous Movile Cave in Romania[9] and Carlsbad Caverns and Lechuguilla Cave in New Mexico were formed this way.

OF THE SEA AND THE GLACIERS

The sea also carves caves as the waves constantly pound on cliffs. Slowly, over long periods of time, the persistent ocean enlarges openings in rock that become caves. Greenland, which is the world's largest island, is mostly located at the north of the Arctic Circle. Greenland is covered by permanent huge ice formations called glaciers that have rugged surfaces, deep cracks, and crevasses. During summer, the sun melts the top layers of glacier ice. Water trickles first and, in time, becomes furious rivers that rush over the surface and fall through crevasses that carve caves inside the ice. Even in these hundreds-of-years-old frozen caves, life has found a way.[10]

Lechuguilla Cave is 122 miles (196 kilometers) long.[11] This type of cave is one of the most extreme environments ever found and home to living creatures not found anywhere else.

LAVA TUBES

Lava can form caves called lava tubes. Kilauea volcano in Hawaii created Kazumura (or Kazamura) Cave. It has more than 41 miles (65.5 kilometers) of passages, which makes it the longest lava cave in the world. Lava tubes form much quicker than solution caves. Kazumura Cave is between 350 and 700 years old.

The process of forming lava caves begins with a volcanic eruption churning out thick streams of magma or liquid lava. Rivers of lava slide down the volcano, and the air begins to cool down the outer layer,

Lava tubes in Hawaii. Notice the roots hanging from the ceiling, which provide a home to insects and other animals.

which then becomes hard. But underneath the hardened surface, lava continues to flow creating a tunnel through which lava flows as long as the volcano spits it out. Once the volcano runs out of lava, the tunnel is empty leaving behind a lava cave.[12]

CAVE FORMATIONS: STALAGMITES, SODA STRAWS, STALACTITES, AND CAVE PEARLS

Caves are much more than empty spaces underground. Water can also sculpt amazing shapes out of calcite. As the calcite solution drips through the cave's ceiling, calcite comes out of solution forming crystals. Grain by grain, calcite crystals fall on the ground and accumulate from the ground up, forming cone structures called stalagmites. Sometimes, calcite crystals shape into long, hollow tubes that hang

Cave pearls formation in Crabtree Cave, Tennessee (above). The stalactites and stalagmites meet to form columns, which can be seen here in Carlsbad caverns, New Mexico (below).

11

from the ceiling called soda straws. When crystals fill the hollow tubes, stalactites form. Round structures called cave pearls form in still pools.[13]

Bizarre creatures live in these amazing extreme cave environments. They have adapted to total darkness, little food, and sometimes to toxic chemicals that would be lethal to most surface creatures.

WATER AND CAVES

There are many caves in all continents, even in Antarctica where fumarole caves form where steam and hot gases emerge through volcanic vents. Water is essential to form most caves and for the survival of cave creatures. Underground water represents 94 percent of all the unfrozen freshwater of the planet. The rest is stored in lakes, rivers, and the atmosphere. About fifty thousand caves have been discovered in the United States and more than one hundred thousand in Europe.[14]

Cave formation in Jackson Cave, Florida. Notice the drops of water at the tips of the formation.

2
WHAT IS IT LIKE LIVING IN A CAVE?

Caves offer three types of environments: the Entrance Zone, the Twilight Zone, and the Deep Cave Zone. At or near the entrance there is usually sunlight, which favors the growth of many plants. Some caves have wide-open entrances that allow plenty of light while others have small openings. Other caves have abundant vegetation or a waterfall covering the entrance. Humidity and temperature varies more than in the other cave zones. Cave entrances usually have more food supplies and more animal life than inside the cave.[1]

THE TWILIGHT ZONE

Light in the twilight zone is very dim. The predominant form of life is a type of bacteria called cyanobacteria, which carry out photosynthesis. Plants that need little light, such as mosses, also live in this zone. It is much cooler and humid. Food is also much less abundant. Most food

The Frick Cave entrance in Georgia is covered with thick vegetation.

comes from outside. Cave visitors, like mice, raccoons, and birds may bring seeds, leaves, fruits, or prey they eat and leave food remains. Water and wind may carry plants and animals. But sometimes food is abundant in certain areas. Guano (bat droppings) and frass (cricket droppings) accumulate and become an important source of food for cave animals, such as beetles and worms.

THE DEEP CAVE ZONE

The habitat deep inside the cave offers extreme conditions. No light reaches this zone, so there are no plants at all. The humidity is high, which means that in many cases animals do not have to worry about dehydration. Many caves are cooler than the outdoors in the summer and warmer in the winter. Food supplies are usually extremely limited. All the animals in the deepest zone are carnivores, or scavengers, eating animal droppings or their remains.[2]

Foxes may use caves as their den or hideout.

Animals living in lava caves may find roots of plants on the surface going through the ceiling of the cave. Many insects live in the roots. Sometimes, water streams find their way inside lava tubes carrying with them a variety of animals and food.

Caves are subterranean ecosystems that are different from other ecosystems because most caves depend on the decomposition of matter. Because there is little or no light reaching inside caves, photosynthesis does not take place below the ground. Subterranean food webs are driven instead by the decomposition of guano, frass, and rotting bodies. These sources of nutrients come from outside the cave.

THE MOST EXTREME CAVE ENVIRONMENTS

Some deep cave environments are extreme not only because they are totally dark and provide little food, but also because they are extremely toxic to most creatures. For example, caves carved by strong acids, such as sulfuric acid, have high amounts of toxic gases like hydrogen sulfide, which smells like rotten eggs.[3]

THE SCENT OF ROTTEN EGGS

Hydrogen sulfide is an invisible gas that prevents cells in the body from using oxygen. This gas quickly affects the nervous system and the heart causing people and animals to pass out and stop breathing.[4]

3
CAVE LIFESTYLES

Cave animals show a variety of lifestyles to adapt to the different environments offered by caves. Most of the animals living at the entrance of caves are visitors. Scientists call them "trogloxenes." Animals, such as bobcats and raccoons, use caves as temporary refuge or shelter at night or during bad weather. Mice, rats, owls, snakes, frogs, lizards, salamanders, as well as spiders and beetles are among the animals that use caves to prey and feed.

LIVING IN THE TWILIGHT ZONE

Other animals make caves an essential part of their life. Many birds nest in caves. For bears, hyenas, and frogs, caves provide a safe place to pass the winter in a dormant state that resembles sleeping. Crickets, frogs, shrimp, salamanders, flatworms, crayfish, wood rats, centipedes, and millipedes live in the twilight zone. Many of these animals also live outside caves in similar environments, so they are called "troglophiles."

A rat shelters her pups in Lowe Gap Cave, Tennessee.

These birds (*Collocalia salagana*) nest in Langs Cave in China.

AMAZING BATS: LIVING UPSIDE DOWN AND IN THE DARK

Bats are one of the best known troglophiles. They sleep inside caves hanging from the ceiling upside down during daytime in summer. They leave the cave at dusk to feed and return at dawn—they are nocturnal, or active at night. Some bats spend winter days and nights inside caves away from harsh weather in a dormant state. Others use caves as a nursery to raise their young.

HOW BATS "SEE": NOSES AND EARS

Bats "see" in the dark by using sound, which is called echolocation. They send out sounds that bounce off objects producing an echo that bats can detect. People cannot hear echolocation signals because they are ultrasonic—too high for human ears to detect. Echoes tell bats where objects are. Bats use this information to avoid obstacles or predators, and to find other bats, food, or a place to roost. Because sound is important for bat's survival, bats have special ears and noses that come in hundreds of different shapes and sizes.[1]

Bat ears concentrate the returning echoes of echolocation calls. Some ears are shaped to detect non-ultrasonic sounds made by prey, such as insect's footsteps. The ears of the well-named long-eared bat of Europe can be three-quarters the length of this thumb-sized bat. Some bats emit echolocation signals through their noses. The noses have odd shapes with leaves or folds that help direct the signals. Some bats have nose leaves as big as their ears.

19

BAT FACTS

✦ Bats are mammals. They have fur and give birth to live young, which they feed milk. (Only two species are furless.)[2]

✦ Bats live everywhere in the world, except Antarctica. Some bat species may live between thirty and forty years.

✦ Bats are the only mammals that fly. Their scientific name is "*Chiroptera*," which in Greek means "hand-winged." Their wings are made of see-through, elastic skin, half the thickness of a human hair. Long fingers support the wing's skin, like the spokes on an umbrella. Thumbs have claws for climbing. Their fingers are made of hollow bones. Lighter bones make flying easier.

✦ Currently, there are about 5,400 species of mammals and about 1,100 of them are bats. (Only rodent species— such as mice and rats—are more numerous than bat species). Some bats are solitary or live alone. Others live in colonies, which can have millions of bats, such as the Mexican free-tailed bat colonies of Texas, Oklahoma, and New Mexico.

✦ Bats are divided into two groups: megabats or big bats, and microbats or small bats. The smallest bat is Thailand's bumblebee bat, which weighs as much as a dime. The largest bat is the flying fox bat. Some flying fox bats attain a wingspan of 5 feet (1.5 meters), with a head and body length of about 16 inches (40 centimeters). However, it only weighs about 3.3 pounds (1.5 kilograms), which is similar to the weight of an adult Chihuahua dog—they weigh between 2 and 6 pounds (1 and 3 kilograms).[3]

✦ Megabats and microbats eat a lot of food—about half their weight or more each night. Flying takes a lot of energy! Most bats are carnivores. They eat animals, mainly insects, such as moths and mosquitoes, and also centipedes, scorpions, birds, fish, lizards, and even other bats. Most megabats are vegetarians. They feast on leaves, fruits, flower nectar, or pollen. Three vampire species live exclusively on blood.

Dog-faced bats roosting together.

The Malayan flying fox bat is the largest bat in the world.

Sound is so important to bats that they learn to use it properly as they grow up. Baby bats babble, like young children do, to learn the right combination of sounds to communicate with other bats.[4]

BAT EYES

Bats that feed on fruits, flower nectar, and pollen use mostly sight to find their food. They tend to have big, round eyes, which can see three times better than people's eyes do. Some fruit bats have eyes with a shiny lining called tapetum, which reflects light and makes it easier to see in dim light.

Bat eyes are for night vision but not for daylight and color vision. Scientists thought bats were completely color blind. However, the eyes of the small flower bat *Glossophaga soricina* are sensitive to ultraviolet (UV) light. It turns out that the flowers the bat feeds on reflect intense UV light. Having UV vision helps these bats find their favorite food in dim light. Only a few other mammals have been found so far to have UV vision. These include several rodents (most, but not all, are nocturnal), a mole, and two marsupials.[5]

Vegetarian bats also use their sense of smell to find food, so their noses are long and pointed. Since they rely mostly on sight and smell to locate food, their ears are usually small. On the other hand, bats that feed on animals rely more on their hearing, so they tend to have small eyes and huge ears.

AMAZING VAMPIRE BATS

Vampire bats fly but they land on the ground to feed on the blood of wildlife or on farm animals, including cows, pigs, chickens, and horses. Vampire bats need to be careful when they feed. They might need to take off quickly if the prey, which is much bigger than they are, tries to brush them off.[6]

SMALL AND LIGHT

Vampire bats are small and light. Their body matches the size of an adult's thumb and they have a wingspan as long as a regular drinking straw (about 8 inches or 20 centimeters). They weigh as much as five

BATS AND DISEASE

Bats may suffer from diseases that also affect people. Rabies and histoplasmosis are the most dangerous diseases bats can pass on to people. A virus causes rabies, and bats sick with rabies may pass on the disease to a person by biting him or her. Histoplasmosis is a fungus that grows in guano. Inhaling airborne fungal spores may infect people. Both diseases are serious, but there are treatments.[7]

WHITE NOSE SYNDROME

White Nose Syndrome (WNS) has killed more than a million bats in the northeastern region of the United States since it was discovered in 2006. WNS is caused by a white fungus that grows on the bat's nose. Bats with WNS wake up more often during their winter dormant state than bats without the disease. When awake, bats consume their fat reserves faster than when they are dormant. They use all their fat reserves before winter is over and die of starvation. No other bat disease has caused as many deaths. Scientists think WNS does not affect people, but they are concerned because bats are an important part of their ecosystem. If bat populations continue to decline, nobody knows how this will affect the ecosystem.

Vampire bats need two tablespoons of blood every day to stay healthy. This vampire bat leaves the cave in search of food.

colored pencils (1 ounce or 28 grams). This is the weight before a meal. Vampire bats need two tablespoons of blood every day to stay healthy. After this meal, they increase their weight to one-and-a-half times their weight before the meal.[8] The extra weight makes the bat too heavy to fly so it waddles off to a safe place to digest before taking off back to the roost.

FINDING FOOD

Vampire bats roost on the ceilings of caves, and in trees, hollow places, and even buildings from the warmest regions of North, Central, and South America. They form colonies of hundreds or thousands of individual bats that leave their home at the darkest time of the night to hunt. They track warm-blooded animals following their scents and sounds, using echolocation and heat sensors. Once they find prey, they land on the ground and waddle toward the legs.

Vampire bats typically roost on the ceilings of caves in the warmest regions of North, Central, and South America. This group of vampire bats hang upside down in a cave in Argentina.

They make a small cut on the skin using a pair of sharp front teeth called incisors. Then, they lap up the flowing blood using their grooved tongue. The blood does not stop flowing because there are chemicals in the bat's saliva to prevent clotting. The victim does not feel a thing either. The saliva carries an anesthetic, or painkiller, that numbs the wound. A single vampire bat cannot take enough blood from one victim to harm it, but the open wounds may get infected. On the other hand, many bats feeding on the same small prey, such as a chicken, may take enough blood to harm it.

TAKING CARE OF EACH OTHER

Vampire bat colonies have strong social bonds, which help them survive. If bats do not drink a daily meal of two tablespoons of blood, they lose weight quickly. Many nights, bats may not get the blood they need. On these occasions, the colony takes care of the hungry bats. Once back in the cave, those bats that had a full meal regurgitate in the mouths of hungry ones and prevent them from starving.

Vampire bats are amazing creatures. However, they are also pests in parts of Mexico and Central and South America. They may also carry the rabies virus, so in some areas they are a health concern.

THE GIANT BAT-EATING CENTIPEDE

Bats have many enemies. Snakes, hawks, falcons, owls, and a South American squirrel monkey prey on bats. Invertebrates, such as cockroaches, ants, beetles, and spiders also include bats in their diet.

But in Cueva del Guano (Guano Cave), which is located in Venezuela, a giant centipede called *Scolopendra gigantea* has an amazing bat-hunting strategy never seen before.[9]

   The Venezuelan scientists reported that they descended through a passage that led into one of the cave's chambers. About 50,000 bats live in the cave. Hanging from the ceiling they saw a 6-inch- (15-centimeter) long *Scolopendra* feeding on a bat. In total darkness,

The poisonous giant centipede, *Scolopendra gigantea*, lives in tropical caves.

the centipede had crawled all the way up and dangled from the ceiling like a trapezist, waiting for bats to pass through. Zap! In an instant, a bat collided with the centipede, but did not knock it down. The centipede clutched the bat and bit it on the neck with its venom-bearing fangs, killing the bat in seconds. The scientists saw evidence that the bat had vigorously tried to free itself from the deadly trap. There was bat hair tangled in the heels, toes, and claws.

But the centipede held on tight. It remained attached to the ceiling with its last five pairs of legs while it held the bat using its first eight pairs of legs. Moving its head from side to side, the centipede was eating a bat that had a wingspan as long as the centipede.

Giant centipedes are common in northern South America and in Trinidad Island. They also feed on other animals, including crickets, snails, worms, cockroaches, lizards, toads, and mice. This centipede is the largest in the world, growing to about 12 inches (30 centimeters) long, just like a regular school ruler.[10]

4
IT'S A TROGLOBITE'S LIFE

It is in the deepest, darkest cave zones that the most bizarre and extreme creatures live. They spend all their lives in the deepest zones; they cannot survive outside the cave. They are called "troglobites."

The looks of a troglobite give away its deep cave dweller lifestyle. Most of them have all or some of the following characteristics: little or no eyes, their bodies are light colored, they have very long bodies, legs, or antennae, and have other senses enhanced. Many invertebrates, such as shrimp-looking amphipods, spiders, and centipedes, have tiny eyes or no eyes at all. They also have very long, thin legs and antennae that guide them through dark surfaces.

By far, invertebrates, such as insects, crustaceans, and arachnids, are the most common kind of animals in the deepest parts of caves. Nevertheless, there are vertebrates, mainly salamanders and fish, that have fascinating troglobite lives. In 1768, Josephus Nicolaus

Arachnids are one of the most common invertebrates found in the deepest parts of caves. This nesticus spider is spinning a web.

Laurenti wrote a scientific description of the first troglobite—the eyeless cave salamander, *Proteus anguinus*, or "Olm."[1] Before Laurenti, popular folklore claimed these blind salamanders were baby dragons.[2]

THE OLM

Proteus anguinus is a blind salamander with a slender body as long as a school ruler and a flattened head. It lives in underground ponds breathing through gills, which resemble the gills in other salamanders.

The olm's large gills allow it to get as much oxygen as possible in the oxygen-deprived underground waters. When oxygen is too low in the water, the olm breathes air using its lungs. The olm is an amphibian related to frogs, newts, and salamanders. Amphibians have a permeable skin through which water and gases, such as oxygen, can pass. The olm lives in caves along the Adriatic Coast in Europe.

SURVIVING IN THE DARK

The olm is very well suited to survive in dark environments. For example, it is capable of finding food by tracking very little amounts of chemical clues. It uses scent sensors inside the nose that are thicker than those of surface amphibians. They also have taste buds on the top of their tongues and at the entrance to the gills, which work together with the nose sensors.

Olms have special sensors inside their ears that detect sound waves in the water as well as vibrations from the ground. They have a lateral line, which consist on a series of sensory cells along its long body. They complement their hearing by detecting low-frequency sounds produced when water is disturbed, for example, by prey splashing.

The olm's head has sensors that detect weak electric fields, like those produced by other animals' bodies. The olm's enhanced sensors work together to detect food, predators, and mates, making up for the lack of vision. Furthermore, scientists have done experiments that show that olms can detect magnetic fields. They may use this ability to find their bearings using Earth's magnetic field.

The Olm is well adapted to survive in dark environments. It searches for food by using scent sensors inside the nose and taste buds on the top of its tongue.

THE CAVE MOLLY AND THE WATER BUG

Fish are one of the few vertebrate species to inhabit deep cave environments. One interesting example is *Poecilia mexicana*, also known as the cave molly. One of the best-studied cave molly populations lives in Cueva del Azufre (Sulfur Cave) in Mexico. The fish in this cave are interesting for two reasons. First, they have adapted to a cave with abundant hydrogen sulfide. Second, they have a predator inside the cave that would not attack them outside the cave.[3]

STARVING FOR OXYGEN

Cave mollies in Cueva del Azufre swim in waters that have high amounts of poisonous hydrogen sulfide, which blocks oxygen uptake. The waters are also poor in oxygen, so mollies strive for the vital gas to stay alive. Mollies are the only fish species in the cave, and, despite the hydrogen sulfide, they are present in relatively abundant numbers.

Scientists were puzzled. How can this fish live in this extremely poisonous environment where other fish do not survive? Most animals living in high-sulfur environments are invertebrates, and the sulfur compounds also poison them. However, invertebrates have a number of strategies to counteract the toxic effects. For example, some simply avoid places with high concentrations. Others have a way to change the sulfide into nonpoisonous forms.[4] It turns out that the cave molly survives in a different way.

Scientists discovered that cave mollies breathe with their gills in the water level right at the border with the surface—this is called aquatic surface respiration. This water level, called the air-water interface, has more oxygen than layers beneath. Breathing more oxygen helps counteract the toxic effect of hydrogen sulfide. However, this strategy has a downside. Cave mollies need to spend so much time breathing at the water surface to get enough oxygen that they have to cut down on their feeding time.[5] Scientists continue studying the cave molly. They want to find out if this amazing fish has other ways to neutralize sulfide compounds.

The cave molly is able to survive in a highly toxic environment with a special breathing technique called aquatic surface respiration.

PREY–PREDATOR ROLES REVERSED

Mollies that live outside caves have two types of predators: birds and other fish. However, inside Cueva del Azufre there are no other fish and no birds. So scientists thought that cave mollies had no predators.

Deep inside caves, the roles of prey and predator are sometimes reversed, just as the giant centipede and the bats in Cueva del Guano. Cave mollies and the giant water bug, *Belostoma,* are an interesting example of a bug hunting a fish. Water bugs are sit-and-wait predators. They lean at the edge of the water from rocks keeping their strong, thick front legs in the water. Upon contact with a molly, they quickly capture it and inject toxins that paralyze the fish. A 1-inch (2.3-centimeters)-long *Belostoma* may catch and eat a molly of the same size or even bigger (1.4 inches or 3.5 centimeters). Living in this extreme environment has led bugs to hunt fish as well as other prey larger than them, such as insects, snails, and frogs.[6]

THE SMALLEST ARE THE TOUGHEST

The smallest organisms are the toughest on the planet. A special type of microorganisms, called extremophiles, are able to tolerate the strongest acids, the most poisonous fumes, the highest and the lowest temperatures, the strongest radiations, and the saltiest environments.

Some of these single-celled organisms belong to a group called Archaea, which is related to bacteria. As its name indicates, Archaea

The *Belastoma* preys on cave mollies. This water bug waits at the edge of the surface to capture the fish

TYPES AND NUMBERS OF TROGLOBITES[7]

TYPE OF ANIMAL	NUMBER OF SPECIES FOUND IN THE WORLD / NUMBER LIVING IN CAVES
PROTOZOANS (SINGLE-CELLED ORGANISMS)	26,000 IN THE WORLD / 360 LIVING IN CAVE WATER OR SOIL
SPONGES	5,000 IN THE WORLD / SEVERAL DOZENS LIVING IN SALT AND FRESH WATER
ANEMONES AND JELLYFISH	10,000 IN THE WORLD / A FEW SPECIES IN CAVES (MOST WITH BURROWING HABITS)
FLATWORMS	25,000 IN THE WORLD / 200 IN CAVES
ROUNDWORMS	20,000 IN THE WORLD / 20 IN CAVES
MOLLUSKS (OYSTERS, SNAILS)	200,000 IN THE WORLD / A FEW HUNDRED IN CAVES
CRUSTACEANS (CRABS, SHRIMP)	52,000 IN THE WORLD / 4,800 IN CAVES
ARACHNIDS (SPIDERS, SCORPIONS)	93,000 IN THE WORLD / 3,000 IN CAVES
MILLIPEDES AND CENTIPEDES	13,000 IN THE WORLD / 300 IN CAVES
INSECTS (SPRINGTAILS, CRICKETS, TERMITES, COCKROACHES, CICADAS, LICE, BEETLES, ANTS, BEES, WASPS, BUTTERFLIES, FLEAS, MOSQUITOES, FLIES)	MORE THAN ONE MILLION IN THE WORLD / MANY THOUSANDS (MAYBE TENS OF THOUSANDS) IN CAVES
FISH	28,000 IN THE WORLD / 299 IN CAVES
AMPHIBIANS (SALAMANDERS)	350 IN THE WORLD / 11 IN CAVES
REPTILES	ONLY TEMPORARY VISITS TO CAVES
BIRDS	10,000 IN THE WORLD / ONLY OILBIRDS AND SWIFLETS USE CAVES EXTENSIVELY
MAMMALS	ONLY BATS (ABOUT 1,100 SPECIES) USE CAVES EXTENSIVELY

CAVE BACTERIA ARE MORE NUMEROUS THAN ANY OF THE GROUPS LISTED ABOVE.

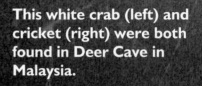

This white crab (left) and cricket (right) were both found in Deer Cave in Malaysia.

are among the oldest living creatures on the planet and perhaps are relatives of the first living species on Earth.[8]

Cave extremophiles play the role plants play outside caves. In certain types of caves with toxic gases like hydrogen sulfide, extremophiles are the producers of the food many troglobites need. The difference is that these microbes do not make food using simple compounds and light (photosynthesis). They power the production of food using energy from chemical reactions that use the toxic compounds in the cave (chemosynthesis). The microbes grow and form gooey mats called biofilms. Biofilms drip from ceilings or stalagmites, or cover the walls, the ground, or the surface of streams. Scientists call these gooey drips "snotites." Other animals in the cave feed on the biofilms creating a new type of ecosystem totally independent of sunlight. These types of biofilms have also been found deep in the ocean around hydrothermal vents and seafloor methane seeps supporting unique deep-sea ecosystems.

Caves are amazing extreme environments inhabited by many living creatures we are barely beginning to understand. It is a fertile field of study in which every year scientists discover more and more secrets of the creatures underground. Would you like to be a scientist of extreme environments?

HANDS-ON ACTIVITY
HOW ACID SHAPES CAVES

In this experiment, you will compare the effects of tap water and a mild acid on calcium carbonate.

MATERIALS

- 2 pieces of sidewalk chalk (*do not* use dustless, washable, or synthetic chalk)

- 2 medium-sized bowls

- Enough white vinegar to cover the chalk in the bowl. (Be careful with the vinegar; wash your hands after the experiments.)

- Enough tap water to cover the chalk in the bowl

- Timer

- Dull knife

- Paper towels

- Spoon

WHAT TO DO

1. Mark one bowl "vinegar" and the other "water."

2. Pour vinegar in the corresponding bowl. Do the same with the water.

3. Divide one piece of chalk into two pieces of about the same size.

4. Place one piece of chalk in the bowl containing vinegar and the other piece in the bowl with water.

5. Observe the pieces of chalk for one minute.

6. What is happening to the chalk in the bowl with vinegar? What is happening to the other piece of chalk?

7. Natural chalk comes from limestone rocks. Vinegar is a mild acid that immediately reacts with limestone (calcium carbonate.) The reaction releases carbon dioxide, a gas that bubbles from the chalk in the bowl with vinegar.

8. After one minute, transfer the pieces of chalk to separate paper towels. (Use a spoon to transfer the chalk in the vinegar bowl.)

9. Try to cut in half each piece of chalk using the dull knife. Which piece of chalk is harder to cut?

CONCLUSION

The reaction between the chalk and the vinegar has weakened the chalk. A similar process occurs in nature leading to the formation of caves.

CHAPTER NOTES

Chapter 1. Enter the Cave World

1. Judith Boogaart, "Stephen Bishop: Cave Explorer," HighlightsKids.com, n.d., <http://www.highlightskids.com/Stories/NonFiction/NF0206_caveExplorer.asp> (June 3, 2011).

2. "Mammoth Cave," U.S. National Park Service, February 2011, <http://www.nps.gov/maca/index.htm> (March 25, 2011).

3. David C. Culver and Tanja Pipan, *The Biology of Caves and Other Subterranean Habitats* (Oxford: Oxford University Press, 2009), p. 5.

4. Ibid., pp. 5–16.

5. William B. White and Elizabeth L. White (eds.), *Karst Hydrology: Concepts From Mammoth Cave Area* (New York: Van Nostrand Reinhold, 1989), pp. 1–3.

6. Culver and Pipan, p. 1.

7. Nancy Holler Aulenbach and Hazel A. Barton with Marfé Ferguson Delano, *Exploring Caves: Journeys into the Earth* (Washington D.C.: National Geographic Society, 2001), p. 45.

8. Mark Twain, *The Adventures of Tom Sawyer,* p. 263, n.d., <http://etext.lib.virginia.edu/etcbin/toccer-new2?id=Twa2Tom.sgm&images=images/modeng&data=/texts/english/modeng/parsed&tag=public&part=29&division=div1> (March 25, 2011).

9. National Science Foundation, "Buried in Romania: Forever-Dark Cave Crawling With Life," Press release, October 24, 1995.

10. Holler Aulenbach et. al., p. 9.

11. "Lechuguilla Cave," U.S. National Park Service, May 27, 2010, <http://www.nps.gov/cave/naturescience/lechuguilla_cave.htm> (March 25, 2011).

12. Culver and Pipan, p. 15.

13. Holler Aulenbach et. al., pp. 37–38.

14. Culver and Pipan, p. 3.

Chapter 2. What Is It Like Living in a Cave?

1. David C. Culver and Tanja Pipan, *The Biology of Caves and Other Subterranean Habitats* (Oxford: Oxford University Press, 2009), p. 40.

2. Ibid., p. 42.

3. Ibid., p. 6.

4. "Medical Management Guidelines for Hydrogen Sulfide (H_2S)," Agency for Toxic Substances and Disease Registry, February 20, 2009, <http://www.atsdr.cdc.gov/MHMI/mmg114.html#bookmark02> (March 25, 2011).

Chapter 3. Cave Lifestyles

1. Aldemaro Romero and Danté Fenolio (Photographer), *Cave Biology Life in Darkness* (Cambridge: Cambridge University Press, 2009), pp. 125–126.

2. Ibid.

3. Hilary Harman, *The Complete Chihuahua Encyclopedia* (New York: Arco Publishing Company, 1972), p. 164.

4. Mirjam Knörnschild, Oliver Behr, and Otto Von Helversen, "Babbling Behavior in the Sac-winged Bat (*Saccopteryx bilineata*)," *Naturwissenschaften*, vol. 93, no. 9, September 2006, p. 453.

5. Brigitte Müller, *et.al.*, "Bat Eyes Have Ultraviolet-Sensitive Cone Photoreceptors," *PLos ONE*, vol. 4, Issue 7, July 2009, p. e6390.

6. Nikki Michel, "The Biogeography of Vampire Bat (*Desmondus rotundus*)," San Francisco State University, 1999, <http://bss.sfsu.edu/geog/bholzman/courses/Fall99Projects/vampire.htm> (March 25, 2011).

7. "Bats and Diseases", Wildlife and Heritage Service, n.d., <http://www.dnr.state.md.us/wildlife/Plants_Wildlife/bats/nhpbatdisease.asp> (March 25, 2011).

8. Michel, "The Biogeography of Vampire Bat (*Desmondus rotundus*)."

9. Jesús Molinari, *et.al.*, "Predation by Giant Centipedes, *Scolopendra gigantea*, on Three Species of Bats in a Venezuelan Cave," *Caribbean Journal of Science*, vol. 41, no. 2, 2005, pp. 340–346.

10. Catherine Meshew, "*Scolopendra gigantea*; giant centipede," *Animal Diversity Web*, 2001, <http://animaldiversity.ummz.umich.edu/site/accounts/information/Scolopendra_gigantea.html> (March 25, 2011).

Chapter 4. It's a Troglobite's Life

1. David C. Culver and Tanja Pipan, *The Biology of Caves and Other Subterranean Habitats* (Oxford: Oxford University Press, 2009), p. 67.

2. "The Dragon Chronicles", PBS.org, 2009, <http://www.pbs.org/wnet/nature/episodes/the-dragon-chronicles/video-full-episode/4563/> (March 28, 2011).

3. Michael Tobler, "Predation of a Cave Fish (*Poecilia Mexicana, Poeciliidae*) by a Giant Water-Bug (*Belostoma, Belostomatidae*) in a Mexican Sulfur Cave," *Ecological Entomology,* vol. 32, 2007, pp. 492–495.

4. Michael Tobbler, "Life on the Edge: Hydrogen Sulfide and the Fish Communities of a Mexican Cave and Surrounding Waters," *Extremophiles,* vol. 10, 2006, pp. 577–585.

5. Michael Tobler, "Compensatory Behavior in Response to Sulphide-induced Hypoxia Affects Time Budget, Feeding Efficiency, and Predation Risk," *Evolutionary Ecology Research,* vol. 11, 2009, pp. 935–948.

6. Tobler, "Predation of a Cave Fish (*Poecilia Mexicana, Poeciliidae*) by a Giant Water-Bug (*Belostoma, Belostomatidae*) in a Mexican Sulfur Cave."

7. Aldemaro Romero and Danté Fenolio (Photographer), *Cave Biology Life in Darkness* (Cambridge: Cambridge University Press, 2009), pp. 76–129.

8. Ibid., p. 54.

GLOSSARY

ARCHAEA • One of the two groups of the oldest living single-celled organisms similar to bacteria.

BIOFILM • A thin layer of cells of microorganisms, such as bacteria.

CARBONIC ACID • A weak acid formed by the combination of water and carbon dioxide.

CAVE • A natural underground chamber.

CREVASSE • A deep crack.

ECHOLOCATION • A means of locating an object by using sound and its echo.

EXTREMOPHILE • Organisms that live in extreme environments.

FRASS • Insect droppings.

FUMAROLE • A vent in a volcanic area through which steam and hot gases emerge.

GUANO • Bat droppings.

HYDROGEN SULFIDE • Poisonous gas that smells like rotten eggs.

KARST • A landscape characterized by rock that can be dissolved by weak acids and form caves and underground streams.

LIMESTONE • Rock made of calcium carbonate from the skeletons and shells of ocean organisms; most caves are in limestone landscapes.

MAGMA • Molten rock deep within Earth; when it flows from a volcano it is called lava.

SPELUNKING • Cave exploration.

STALACTITE • A conical cave formation made of limestone that slowly grows from the cave ceiling down.

STALAGMITE • A conical cave formation made of limestone that slowly grows from the cave floor up.

SULFURIC ACID • A strong acid formed by the combination of water and hydrogen sulfide.

TROGLOBITE • Animals that live in the deepest, darkest parts of caves permanently.

TROGLOPHILE • Animals that live part of their lives in caves, but can also live outside caves.

TROGLOXENE • Animals that are temporary visitors of caves.

FURTHER READING

Books

Cooper, Sharon K. *Caves and Crevices*. Chicago: Heinemann-Raintree, 2009.

Costain, Meredith. *Into the Earth: The Story of Caves*. Washington, D.C.: National Geographic, 2006.

Jackson, Donna M. *Extreme Scientists: Exploring Nature's Mysteries From Perilous Places*. Boston: Houghton Mifflin Books for Children, 2009.

Smith, J. Jaye. *Batty About Texas*. Gretna, La.: Pelican Publishing Company, 2009.

Internet Addresses

NATIONAL CAVES ASSOCIATION
  <http://cavern.com/>

NOVA / PBS: THE MYSTERIOUS LIFE OF CAVES
  <http://www.pbs.org/wgbh/nova/caves/>

U.S. NATIONAL PARK SERVICE:
  MAMMOTH CAVE NATIONAL PARK
  <http://www.nps.gov/maca/index.htm>

ANA MARÍA RODRÍGUEZ'S HOMEPAGE

INDEX